Contents

No traffic allowed

A town is busy with people and traffic.

Why is no traffic allowed on the main shopping street?

Street cleaning

The streets are kept clean.
There are litter bins for
people to put their rubbish.

The street cleaner's machine washes the pavements and sweeps up dirt and rubbish.

Inside and outside

This is the shopping centre.
Inside there are 86 shops
and restaurants.

Outside, you walk along pavements and cross roads to get to the shops. Do you like shopping in a shopping centre, or at shops on the street?

Market place

Follow the sign to the market place.
Do you think the merry-go-
round is always there?

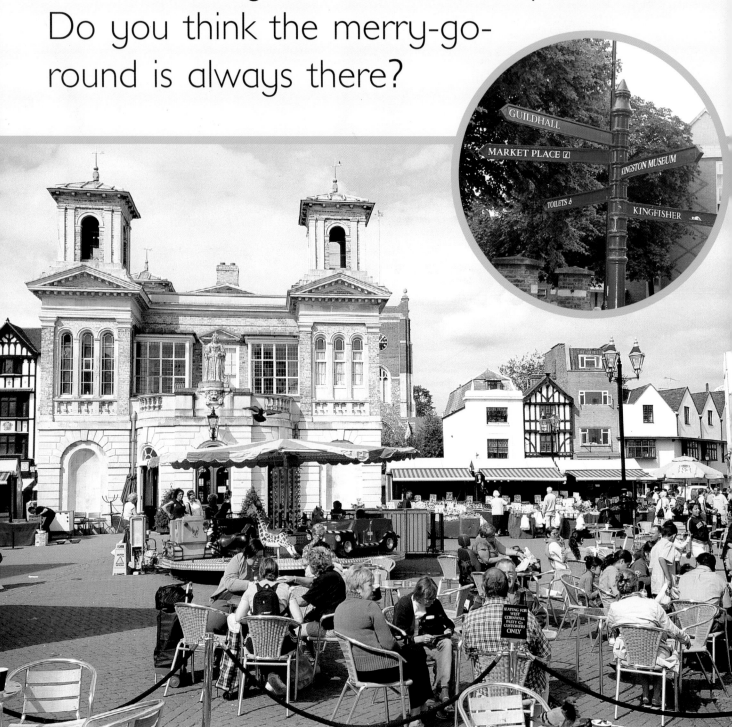

This market stall sells fresh food.
The fruit and vegetables look
and smell delicious!

Bridge over the river

A bridge crosses the river that flows through the town. Steps take you down to the riverside - and up again!

There is a footpath, a cycle track
and a road over the bridge.

Money to spend

A big bank stands in
the town centre.

You don't have to go inside to get out some money.

Crossing the road

Traffic stops while people cross the road at the pedestrian crossing.

What tells the traffic to stop?

A bus full of people stops at the crossing. They might be coming to shop in the town, or just be passing through.

Old and new

Old and new buildings stand side by side.
An old building contains a new shop.

A big new cinema can show
14 different films at once.

Look up!

Look up! What can you see above the busy street? A church clock and old street lamps.

Patterns and ornaments on top of buildings.

A golden statue and a lion's head.

What else might you see?

Going home

A little park is a quiet place to rest after a busy day in the town.
Now it's time to go home.

A timetable tells you the time
your train leaves. What other
ways could you get home?

Map

You can start a walk from any point on a map. To follow the walk in this book, put your finger on **Start** and trace the route.

Key

 pedestrian area

 bench

 shopping centre

 market place

 bridge

 bank

 cinema

 park

 church

 bus stop

 railway station

 parking

Start

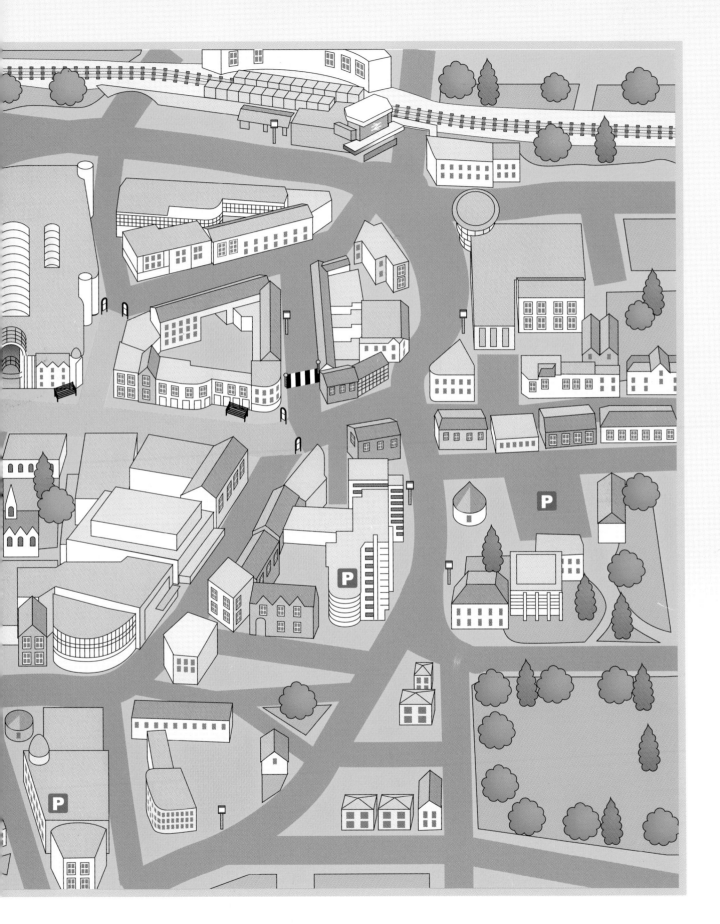

Quiz

It's important to keep the town clean.
How are the streets kept clean?

Look at pages 8 and 9.

There are fruit and vegetable stalls in the market place.
What else is in the market place?

Look at pages 12 and 13.

A river flows through the town.
How can you cross the river?

Look at page 15.

A bank stands on the
main street.
What other buildings
are there in the town?

Look all through the book.

The roads are busy with
traffic.
How can you cross the
road safely?

Look at pages 18 and 19.

You can rest in a little park.
Where else can you sit and
rest in the town?

Look all through the book.

Index